CREATING A CULTURE

THE
COURAGE
CHALLENGE
WORKBOOK

CINDY SOLOMON

To Cindy —
Poll the Lord !

"*Life is either a daring adventure
or nothing.*"

—Helen Keller

FIRST EDITION

Published by OPR Publishers
112 Elsie Street, San Francisco, CA 94110

Interior Design by 1106 Design
Cover Design by ISCA Design

Publisher's Cataloging-in Publication Data

Solomon, Cindy.
Creating a Culture of Courage™: The Courage Challenge Workbook / Cindy Solomon;—
1st ed. p. cm.
    ISBN 978-0-9826728-1-5 (alk. paper)
        1. Courage. 2. Leadership. 3. Change Management

Contents

About The Author

Fifteen years ago, after working her way up to the senior management level in corporate America, Cindy Solomon took a giant leap. She quit her job and embarked on a research project studying the dynamics of courage among the ranks of American businesspeople. She conducted scores of one-on-one interviews. Analyzed the results of numerous in-depth questionnaires. And spent long hours on secondary research.

All of this effort resulted in some surprising conclusions about how we view and use courage to achieve our life, career, and organizational objectives. Those conclusions launched Solomon's first major entrepreneurial venture, *Cindy Solomon & Associates, Inc.,* a speaking and consulting company that has since transformed the way leaders in thousands of national and international organizations make decisions and serve customers. Additional research on the evolving definition of customer service broadened the company's offering and laid the groundwork for Solomon's 2010 best-seller, *The Rules of Woo: Capturing the Hearts & Minds of Today's Customers.*

Today, nationally recognized speaker, trainer, author, and executive consultant Cindy Solomon remains dedicated to ensuring that we all fulfill our innate potential to lead with confidence and make a lasting, positive impact on our teams, organizations, and our customers. Solomon's content-rich keynote speeches and workshops are carefully customized to sync with the needs of individual audiences. And her poignant insights, hilarious real-life stories, and actionable advice on the subjects of Customer Service and Courageous Leadership have made her a popular choice for a wide range of industries.

Solomon has been the #1-rated speaker at events for Oracle, Genentech, Cisco, UPS, the American Automobile Association, and Raytheon, among many others. She has been an annual headliner for Microsoft, Prudential, KeyBank, Telluride Ski & Golf Resort, and the Governor's Conferences for Women in Texas, Pennsylvania, Massachusetts, and New York, (to name just a few). Solomon is also a co-founder of The Women's Success Forum and serves on the board of directors for the Professional BusinessWomen of California. Her insights have appeared worldwide in business and consumer magazines and blogs, and in numerous books by fellow authors, including *The Naked Truth, Women on Top, The Transparency Edge,* and *Extreme Excellence. The Rules of Woo: An Entrepreneur's Guide to Capturing the Hearts & Minds of Today's Customers* is currently available at amazon.com. A second book, *Creating a Culture of Courage: The New Leadership Challenge*, is due out in 2011.

"Courage is like any other muscle ... it is strengthened by use."

—Ruth Gordon

Introduction

I t wasn't so long ago that I sat night after night in my hard-won corner office trying to find new ways to get my team members inspired and fully engaged in our company's objectives. What tools and skills could I provide that would lead them to greatness? As an entrepreneur, that task has grown exponentially. Now instead of teams of familiar faces from just one corporation, I am challenged with inspiring audiences made up of thousands of leaders – as well as individual contributors – from every industry imaginable. Moreover, each organization, division, team, and individual has a unique set of circumstances and a stunning array of modern-world obstacles that need to be overcome.

As I set out to write this workbook, it occurred to me that – whether we work in large multinational corporations or run our own businesses as I do now – the challenges we face have become more complex. Business, heck, life in general, is happening in a condensed time-frame. With immediate access to gobs of information tucked in every corner of the internet, consumers are demanding better, faster, and more individualized attention. Machines can actually "print" three-dimensional products and have them on the market within days of coming off the drawing board (ahem, computer screen). This means competitors can now come from anywhere. At any time.

What on earth is going to keep us from spinning out of control? What will give us the agility and ability to take on the challenges of this new world order? What is the missing skill? Admittedly I'm biased, but I'd say it's courage. Courage can turn a disaster into an opportunity. Courage can empower us to make decisions before all of the data has been collected and analyzed. It can transform our fear of the unknown into a tremendous motivator. A motivator for us, for our teams, for our organizations. Courage can ensure we not only survive, but also thrive.

But what if you don't consider yourself particularly courageous? Is courage something you can learn? I believe it is. I believe we all have courage skills. We simply need to become more aware of them and practice using them consciously. I believe that, once we get used to using them, we can accomplish just about anything. We can provide the fresh thinking that turns uncertainty into opportunity. We can embrace the trial and error process required to make improvements in the way we and our teams work. We can fully engage the minds and hearts of the four different generations in our workplaces. I believe we are capable of these things because of the following "truths" about courage that were brought to light, and are continually reinforced, by my ongoing research study.

What We Know

*1. **Courage Is Personal***—Courage is as unique as each one of us. An action that requires great courage from you might be remarkably easy for someone else. And vice versa. No one can tell you what actions will require courage for you. And, as hard as you try, you can't simply talk someone else into being courageous.

*2. **Courage Is Not What You Think***—Only about 50 percent of us are willing to admit publicly that we are courageous. The rest of us are afraid to make that pronouncement even though we demonstrate courage on a daily basis. Moreover, because of societal norms in the United States and in many other countries, women are even less likely than men to acknowledge their capacity for courage in front of others. And men are more likely to boast of courage prowess even if they don't believe it themselves.

*3. **Courage Is Not A Super Power***—The truth is, courage doesn't usually equal heroism. Only a fraction of the instances we think of as requiring courage actually involve physical endangerment. Courage is less often about being superhuman and more often about what we would consider more common or mundane decisions like how to launch a new business effort or how to handle a tough employee.

*4. **Courage Can Be Learned***—Courage is simply another skill we can choose to learn and develop, like speaking another language or operating a new computer program. We are all born with the capacity to be courageous. The more you use your courage skills, the stronger they become. And just as with physical strength, if you don't use them, you lose them.

5. *Courage Feels Fantastic*—It's why we like horror films and roller coasters. It's why we get charged up when we're given a new and challenging project. It's why they (whoever *they* are) tell you to "do something that scares you every day." On the other end of a courageous act, whether you succeed or fail, there's an achievement high that simply can't be beat. It can help you build your business or go after a new challenge with excitement and gusto. (And people wonder why I love this topic.)

This workbook helps you figure out what courage means for you. It helps you choose a courage challenge that tests and hones your courage skills. And it takes you through a structured framework for working through that challenge ... all the way to that awesome and exhilarating feeling on the other end.

Who Should Use This Workbook?

This workbook is for anyone who is searching for new ways to create or build a career, a team, a company, an organization, or even an industry. It's for everyone whose forward momentum has been slowed or even stymied by fear, indecision, or lack of clear direction. It's for sole proprietors, frontline personnel, office warriors, and even those with assigned parking places, corner offices, and multi-national concerns. It's a tool with, I hope, useful exercises that enable you to leap over hurdles and break through the walls that are keeping you from moving forward with confidence and determination.

Leaders of teams, whether those teams include direct reports or are made up of ad hoc task force members, will find this workbook especially useful. As owners, managers, and directors we've all been asked at some point by our higher-ups or our boards to take more risks, be more innovative. Then they pat us on the shoulder and send us on our way. Ultimately, they are asking us to be more courageous and help those around us to do the same. But you can't just *tell* a team of people to be more courageous. You have to plant and nourish the skills necessary to bring about smart risk taking and courageous innovation. You have to create a culture of courage by modeling the behaviors yourself and consciously enabling your team to do the same.

As leaders, building our teams' courage skills isn't just a personal choice, it's our job. And when we do that job well, it feels fantastic, amazing, maybe even noble.

I hope, no matter what you do for a living, this workbook will help you embrace your full potential as a leader in this exciting and complex world and wield your courage skills in ways that you never imagined possible.

Cindy Solomon
San Francisco, CA
April 2011

"The future belongs to those who believe in the beauty of their dreams."

—Eleanor Roosevelt

Chapter 1

How To Use This Workbook

This workbook is designed to take you through a specific business challenge that you believe is holding your career, your team, or your organization back from the greatness it could be experiencing. It is intended to help you identify, clarify, and then take action or follow through on a series of actions—not without fear but *in spite of* your fears.

At some point in our lives we've all said, "I wish I had the courage to...." This workbook helps you turn those wishes into action. Like any other skill—courage requires that you pay attention, understand what is and isn't working, and create a plan to improve and build upon that skill. You can't simply wish to have more courage. You have to be crystal clear about what it is you are trying to accomplish. You have to understand the barriers you'll face. And you have to create and follow through on a solid strategy that gets you where you want to go. This workbook helps you to ask yourself the right questions and then provides a framework you can use over and over again to create the life, the career, the company you have always wished you had the courage to create.

Each chapter contains critical questions you need to ask yourself to get to the heart of the matter and discover a workable path to success. These questions will help you prioritize the tactics you will need to overcome your fears and defy the obstacles. Some questions may take a bit more mulling over than others. So have patience and avoid skipping steps or cruising over the more difficult tasks. In the end, the work you put into your courage challenge will be equal to the results you get out of it.

You can tackle the entire workbook in a couple of days or over the course of a year. You can use it for a single challenge that has been holding you back. You can also apply the framework again and again as you integrate your "courage skills" into your everyday life. You might find it easier to use this workbook to take on a smaller challenge first. That's okay. Once you have the framework down, you can apply it to a meatier challenge. Or vice versa. The bottom line is, use it. Write in it, scribble in it, photocopy pages and post them in your office. Share it with your friends and colleagues. Do whatever you need to do to make it work for you.

In the next chapter, you're going to begin the process by choosing a "courage challenge." To make sure you get as much as you can out of this process, it might help to consider the following general tips…

TIP #1: Be Realistic & Constructive

Ideally, the courage challenge you choose should be something that doesn't risk the entire company or your livelihood but does help move your career or organization forward in a substantial way. In other words, success will come from being constructive and realistic from the very start.

Too unrealistic or destructive…

I wish I had the courage to finally tell that guy off!

I wish I had the courage to tell my team how badly I think they're doing on this project.

I wish I had the courage to take out my competitor once and for all.

I wish I had the courage to fire all our clients and start over.

More like this...

I wish I had the courage to ask for a raise.

I wish I had the courage to ask permission to manage that project I see floundering.

I wish I had the courage to propose this new strategy or product line.

I wish I had the courage to break with a specific industry norm.

I wish I had the courage to seek a line of credit to build my business.

TIP #2: Make it Energizing & Uncomfortable

You'll know you are on the right path when you feel energized and probably a little uncomfortable. It's important to recognize and embrace that feeling of energized discomfort. That feeling is at the heart of everything great that was ever accomplished in our world. You are onto something when you say to yourself, "Okay, I'm writing this down but I don't really want to have to deal with it. It's too scary. Too much could go wrong. I could make a real mess. But if I were to succeed … it could be a game changer."

If you don't feel any discomfort, then you may be considering something that doesn't really require courage. You may simply need more time, more focus, or more assistance with the task. If that's the case, consider choosing a different challenge.

Too small or mundane...
I wish I had the courage to revise my resume.
I wish I had the courage to get that project finished.
I wish I had the courage to increase our product output.
I wish I had the courage to do some advertising.

More like this...
I wish I had the courage to go for that international
    assignment.
I wish I had the courage to resolve that conflict with a
    difficult team member.
I wish I had the courage to aggressively go after a
    new role.

I wish I had the courage to aggressively partner with
our competition.
I wish I had the courage to package my business for
franchising.

TIP #3: Be Clear & Specific

Choosing a challenge that's too broad or fraught with
too much emotion can be a deal breaker too. As we said
previously, feeling uncomfortable can give you some
clues about whether your challenge is appropriate, but
be careful not to push that emotion too far ... or to
avoid dealing with your emotions altogether by choosing
something vague or all-encompassing.

Your courage challenge should cause healthy discomfort,
not paralyze you with fear. It should be substantive but
not completely wacky. It should cause people to smile
and nod their heads in solidarity rather than shake their
heads in dismay. And it should be clear and specific
enough that you can visualize the end result.

Too broad or wacky...

I wish I had the courage to change my whole life.
I wish I had the courage to try something different.

I wish I had the courage to run away to Tahiti.
I wish I had the courage to wrestle an alligator for
  charity.

More like this...

I wish I had the courage to pitch my new product idea
  to my boss.
I wish I had the courage to challenge the team with a
  significant goal.
I wish I had the courage to bite the bullet on that new
  IT system.
I wish I had the courage to reorganize the team with-
  out regard to tenure or my personal relationships.
I wish I had the courage to pursue a buyer for my
  business.

With these tips in mind, you're ready to get started on the
path to defining your courage challenge and conquering
it with the cool confidence of a pro.

"Have the courage to write down your dream for yourself."

—May Sarton

Chapter 2

CHOOSING A COURAGE CHALLENGE

As we just learned, a great courage challenge is rational and constructive. It's energizing and a bit uncomfortable. And it's clear and specific enough that you can visualize the end result. Much of the battle is in finding the "heart" of the courage challenge you're considering. Doing so may seem like an insurmountable challenge in and of itself, but it's actually quite simple. Just keep asking yourself "why" this particular challenge is important to you, your team, your business, etc.

For example, if you wish you had the courage to ask for a raise, consider *why* you want that raise. What you are really after may not be the extra hundred dollars per paycheck. It may be more about getting the recognition you feel you deserve for a job well done, the acknowledgment that you have a meaningful role in the organization.

If you wish you had the courage to switch to a new IT system, ask yourself what the new IT system will do for your company. What advantages will you have that you don't have now? What will it allow you to achieve or accomplish? Why should you be the one to implement the system? Once you hit the heart of the challenge you'll have a better idea of your motivations and be better prepared to overcome the obstacles that have kept you from making the leap in the past.

Okay, let's get going! One of the most common reasons for not finishing what we start is taking on something we're really not in a position to control—believing that enthusiasm and momentum alone will ensure success if we go for broke or try to take on the whole world in one big, bold leap. The way to avoid going too big or tackling something you don't really have control over is to start by getting all those big ideas out of your head and onto paper. Here's an exercise to help you do that.

EXERCISE 1: WHAT'S THE BIG DEAL?

Use the space below to make a list of the larger issues and high level forces that are at play in your business or industry. These are the big things that are affecting your organization overall. They may be driven by outside forces (e.g., a change in the industry, marketplace, a new competitor entering the space) or they could be issues over which your organization has direct or indirect control (e.g., customer processes, profitability, product offerings, or pricing).

External Forces:

Think about your industry/business/team/workgroup. List all of the significant challenges to your organization from *outside* forces ... economy, industry, competitive challenges, etc.

Internal Forces:

Now, list the greatest *internal* challenges to your situation or your team's ability to achieve its objectives … turf issues, internal politics, lack of resources, confusing or conflicting goals, etc.

EXERCISE 2: SEEING THE OPPORTUNITIES

Now take a look at the potential upside to all those difficult challenges you just jotted down. This exercise will help you to look beyond the toll the lack of action is taking on your business/team/career to the possibilities and opportunities that taking action might bring about.

External Opportunities:

What are the best-case opportunities created by the external forces you wrote down? What is a positive outcome for your team/organization these opportunities create?

What would you or your organization need to do (tactically, culturally, etc.) to take advantage of these opportunities? Are there things you could do to make those opportunities come alive?

Internal Opportunities:

What opportunities are created by the internal forces you wrote down? In your mind, what are the greatest opportunities for your team/organization over the next year?

What would you or your organization need to do (tactically, culturally, etc.) to take advantage of these?

EXERCISE 3: BRINGING IT DOWN TO EARTH

Now that you have your global perspective and the potential opportunities in mind, you are ready to refine your focus a bit. Thinking about the specific ways you could address those issues, use the space on the next page to make a list of the things you wish you had the courage to tackle or accomplish to leverage the opportunities.

Take your time making this list. Be sure to be specific and realistic. Some challenges might be as subtle as trying out a different leadership style with a new employee or colleague. Others might be as dramatic as abandoning a marketing strategy in the middle of a campaign and admitting that it was the wrong direction to go. Or as simple and small as confronting a peer who bullies you or with whom you disagree. Still others might be as momentous as standing up to your board of directors regarding a flaw you see in their strategic direction. Remember, if an idea elicits nervousness, write it down. In this instance, sweaty palms can be a really good sign.

 My specific opportunities are...

EXERCISE 4: CHOOSE YOUR CHALLENGE

Of the opportunities you listed, circle the one that would make the greatest difference to your career/team/organization. Write your chosen challenge in the space below.

 My courage challenge is...

EXERCISE 5: TEST YOUR CHALLENGE

Before you finalize your decision, put your challenge to a simple test. Ask yourself why this particular feat is important to your career, your team, or your organization. Ask yourself if the challenge adheres to the tips we learned in Chapter 1. And finally, clarify the end results you are hoping to see when you succeed.

 This challenge is important because…

Check the boxes below that apply to your challenge...

☐   Is it constructive as opposed to destructive?

☐   Is it realistic as opposed to emotional?

☐   Does it elicit nervousness?

☐   Can you envision a positive end result?

☐   Is it clear as opposed to vague and hazy?

☐   Is it specific as opposed to too broad?

☐   Does it energize and excite you?

What are the best-case-scenario end results? Who will be positively affected? How? What beneficial effects will success have on your career, team, division, or organization?

Congratulations! You've made it over the first big hurdle to conquering your courage challenge. That's right, you picked one. But not just any one. You took your big, scary, amorphous ideas and turned them into a real, tangible challenge that involves using courage to create positive momentum. In doing this, you set a realistic context for what success might actually look like. Now, you are ready to consider the courage skills you will need to conquer your challenge.

"Success doesn't come to you. You go to it."

—Marva Collins

Chapter 3

THE FOUR TYPES OF COURAGE

As with most topics related to human endeavors, courage is a subject that can take years to fully comprehend. In the context of this workbook, we'll stick to the aspects that will be most useful in helping you achieve your desired outcome. Let's start by taking a look at Figure 1. In this chart you'll notice that courage can be broken down into four distinct types.* Each type can be defined and categorized by considering where it falls on the crossroads between two continuums: personal accountability and self-awareness.

* Source: *The Courageous Leadership Study,* performed on an ongoing basis since 1995 by Cindy Solomon & Associates, Inc.

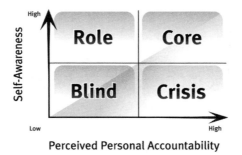

Figure 1: The Courage Quadrants™

Perceived personal accountability is about how much attention you are paying to your own actions and the (real or perceived) effect they could have on you, your situation, the situation of those around you. Self awareness is about how cognizant you are of your values, skills, and knowledge or those of your team or organization when you make a decision to act. Figure 1 shows the four quadrants created by the crossroads between these continuums and the type of courage that lies within each.

BLIND COURAGE

Blind Courage is the kind of courage kids have. It's that crazy, not-paying-attention, "What were you thinking??!!" kind of courage. Picture a child or teenager flying down a hill on a bicycle or a snowboard with no regard for the consequences of falling or getting hurt. Blind Courage can also be exemplified in the "leap of faith" of an entrepreneurial venture.

Blind Courage seems foolhardy yet it's a necessary and integral part of what makes many individuals, leaders, and businesses successful. Think about that umpteenth meeting you just had on a particular project. The one in which you were dying to burst forth with, "Let's just go for it! What's the worst that could happen?" Blind Courage allows you to move quickly to take advantage of opportunities that might otherwise pass you by. It also allows you to quickly sidestep your fears before they lead to inaction.

What Blind Courage looks like:
- You say, "That sounds like fun!" … a lot.
- You feel as though you simply "closed your eyes and jumped."

- You have very little fear of failure, because you aren't considering the consequences.

Blind Courage works *for* you:
- when you are working in your area of expertise;
- when you need to act quickly, with limited data, to take advantage of market opportunities; and/or
- when you (or your team) are stuck in analysis paralysis and time is slipping away.

Blind Courage works *against* you:
- when your excitement over "jumping" keeps you from focusing on the right priorities long enough;
- when you become addicted to it and use it just to feel the rush; and/or
- when you don't follow up with a continuing commitment to the project, strategy, etc.

CRISIS COURAGE

Sometimes Crisis Courage doesn't even feel like a courageous act because, under most circumstances, it's completely instinctual. Crisis Courage is used in perceived life-or-death situations. If you have ever "almost" been in an accident or had someone scare you so much that your adrenaline rushes through your body, you know the feeling that drives Crisis Courage. The physical ramifications of that adrenal rush keep your head from really engaging and you bee-line it to your "fight or flight" mode.

The good news is that this type of courage allows you to, for a short time, achieve a level of performance you never knew you were capable of reaching. The bad news is, those levels aren't sustainable … even if the perceived life-or-death situation continues. Throughout time, many leaders have attempted to create and maintain a motivated workforce by stretching their workers to their very limits and holding them precariously at the edge of a cliff. The initial rush creates a temporary jump in productivity. Unfortunately, once that initial rush is over, burnout ensues.

What Crisis Courage looks like:
- You are in a perceived "life-or-death" situation accompanied by a rush of adrenaline.
- You feel lightheaded, confused, as though you are taking action without conscious thought.
- You may not remember the details of the event or your actions afterward.

Crisis Courage works *for* you:
- when you need to respond to an immediate threat to your wellbeing or that of your team; and/or
- when inaction would cause the demise of your career, team, or organization.

Crisis Courage works *against* you:
- when you employ it for sustained periods of time to the point of burnout;
- when you use it repeatedly, just to feel the adrenaline rush; and/or
- when you put yourself in crisis situations that otherwise could have been avoided.

ROLE COURAGE

Role Courage is one of the most important and yet often overlooked types of courage. It is the confidence and "fearlessness" you experience when you fully understand the part you play in a particular situation and the implied power and responsibility that comes with it. It comes from education, training, and experience. An example of Role Courage might be a trapeze artist who seems to defy death with every leap. To someone untrained in the trapeze arts, it would be too terrifying to consider without a harness and a sturdy net. To the artist, it is a job that he or she has learned so well that execution appears effortless.

Other examples might include a surgeon operating on someone's heart or a lawyer defending a client in front of a judge and jury. In a business setting, being well trained for your role allows you to use Role Courage to make the best decisions for your career, your team, your organization, and/or your customers or clients. Said another way, Role Courage allows you to make decisions and take actions without the fear of failure you might have if you were lacking the special training and knowledge required for that role.

What Role Courage looks like:
- You act with confidence and fearlessness doing what you were "trained" to do.
- You "just know" the right path to take because it is your responsibility to do so.
- Your experience or training allows you to see the path to success that someone without your training might not see.

Role Courage works *for* you:
- when you need to solve a problem or take advantage of an opportunity in your area of expertise;
- when you need to focus on the real priorities and act from a high level of competence and confidence; and/or
- when you believe no one else is better prepared for the challenge at hand than you or your team.

Role Courage works *against* you:

- when you become unable to work across varying areas of expertise because you have competence in only one area;
- when you become fearful of taking action because you don't have "enough" training;
- when you/your team become divided from other areas of the business because of a commitment to a narrow area of expertise; and/or
- when your belief in your own training blinds you to the possibility that someone else who has a higher level of training in the same area might be better suited for the task.

CORE COURAGE

Core Courage is one of the most difficult types of courage to use as it requires a crystal clear understanding of not only where you are currently, but also where you want to go. It requires you to take the time to fully comprehend and commit to a specific outcome. Core Courage is also unique because, once the consequences of your decision have been well considered, it requires you to make a fully formed decision to act, or not act. There's no leaping here.

Moreover, if you determine that the consequences of your action could be negative, Core Courage doesn't compel you to choose inaction. On the contrary, this type of courage requires not only an understanding of the positive and negative consequences, but also an acceptance of either outcome. This type of courage is exemplified by your ability to learn from the results of the outcome, which in turn informs your future decisions. If you've ever worked for a leader who has a vision for the organization and encourages everyone to make a meaningful contribution with regard to how you will achieve that vision, you have experienced the use of Core Courage.

What Core Courage looks like:

- You've taken the time to create a vision for where you want to take your career, your team, your organization, your project, etc.
- You are so confident in your vision that you are completely open to having those around you contribute ideas and opinions to reach the best possible path toward your goal.
- You not only welcome dissenting opinions, but also rely on them as a constant reality check for your vision and the path toward it.

Core Courage works *for* you:

- when you are looking for inspired movement toward a difficult or long-term goal;
- when you are in a crisis and need to create calm and focus within a team or organization;
- when you need to inspire a group of people to find a truly innovative solution; and/or
- when your values as an organization or industry are tested.

Core Courage works *against* you:

- when immediate action is required and there is no time to study your options;
- when you allow the process of discovery to cause analysis paralysis; and/or
- when others on your team have training that would enable them to act from Role Courage but you hold them back because you want to consider all the options first.

As you read through these four types of courage, some of them may have sounded familiar. Maybe even a specific situation comes to mind in which you or someone around you exhibited a certain type of courage. As you become more familiar with the courage types – and begin to see how you and your colleagues are already employing them – you will begin to move from unconscious courage to conscious courage.

EXERCISE 6: YOUR EXPERIENCE WITH COURAGE

Thinking about the four types of courage, ask yourself when you, or someone you know, has employed them to make an important decision or overcome an obstacle.

Blind Courage

 The situation was…

 The action I took/saw someone else take was…

 I knew it was Blind Courage because…

Crisis Courage

 The situation was…

 The action I took/saw someone else take was…

 I knew it was Crisis Courage because…

Role Courage

 The situation was…

 The action I took/saw someone else take was…

 I knew it was Role Courage because…

Core Courage

 The situation was…

 The action I took/saw someone else take was…

 I knew it was Core Courage because…

If you are like most people, you thought of several instances for each type of courage. That's because we are all acting courageously every single day. The more you look around and recognize the types of courage and how we all use them, the better you'll be able to see the subtle nuances that allow you to make conscious choices about which type(s) of courage you need to achieve your goals. Now, you are ready to begin applying the four types of courage to the challenge you chose in Chapter 2. You are ready to turn the theory into action.

*"Life shrinks or expands
in proportion to one's courage."*

—Anaïs Nin

Chapter 4

USING COURAGE
CONSCIOUSLY

As we said previously, we all use all four kinds of courage every day … at home, in our careers, with our teams. Even whole companies and organizations make courageous moves that are born out of the four types of courage. But simply using courage isn't what creates success. What creates success is the ability to see how, and in what situations, you should apply each type of courage. To consciously choose the type of courage that is most likely to result in the desired outcome. The best way to bring about this consciousness and clarity is to apply each type of courage to your challenge to see how it fits.

Example: Getting funding for a business venture

Blind Courage: Blurt it out one day while having lunch with a venture capitalist.

Crisis Courage: Do whatever it takes to find the money fast—even mortgage the house.

Role Courage: Use years of training in sales to overcome the VC's objections.

Core Courage: Put together a value-based proposal that demonstrates how the venture will be profitable for the VC and seek out VCs who are a good fit with those values.

EXERCISE 7: SEEING WHAT FITS

Use the spaces on the following pages to see how the different types of courage may fit with your challenge.

Blind Courage

 How might you use Blind Courage to conquer your challenge? What would the "leap of faith" look like?

 If your challenge involves a group, team, or entire organization, how could Blind Courage be used to take advantage of the opportunities?

 What is a realistic best-possible-scenario if you were to use Blind Courage for this challenge?

Crisis Courage

How might you use Crisis Courage to spur yourself to action? What would an act of Crisis Courage look like in response to your courage challenge?

If your challenge involves a group, team, or entire organization, how might Crisis Courage be used to take advantage of the opportunity?

What is a realistic best-possible-scenario if you were to use Crisis Courage for this challenge?

Role Courage

How might Role Courage apply to your challenge? What education, training, knowledge and experience do you have that might allow you to act in a way that others without such training might not be able to act?

If your challenge involves a group, team, or entire organization, how might Role Courage – or the training and experience they possess – be used to take advantage of the opportunities?

What is a realistic best-possible-scenario if you were to use Role Courage for this challenge?

Core Courage

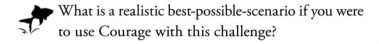 If you decided to use Core Courage to conquer your challenge, what sort of a discovery process would you employ? At what point would you know what you needed in order to take action?

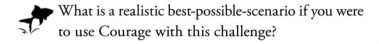 If your challenge involves a group, team, or entire organization, how might Core Courage – or analysis and exploration of values and options – be used to take advantage of the opportunities?

 What is a realistic best-possible-scenario if you were to use Courage with this challenge?

As you worked through the previous exercise, you may have noticed that more than one type of courage could be used to achieve your desired outcome. Often, if your challenge involves a team or the organization at large, the type of courage you'll need as a leader may be different from the type of courage your team or organization members will need to implement the action.

For example, you may need Core Courage to launch a new initiative, but your team may need training or Role Courage to get the job done. Another example is, your team may draw upon Role Courage to take action, but you may need Blind Courage to give them the permission and space they need to act.

EXERCISE 8: LOOKING AT THE UPSIDE

Take a minute now to review your courage-use scenarios. If you looked only at the realistic best case scenarios, which type of courage would you employ for yourself? For your team? Said another way, if you set aside your fears and concerns completely … which type of courage do you need to move forward on your courage challenge? Remember, it may be more than one type.

 What type of courage do *you* most need to move effectively toward success against your challenge?

 What type of courage would your team/organization need?

If you were required to take action right now using the type(s) of courage you wrote in the previous questions, what would be your first three steps toward conquering your courage challenge?

Are you beginning to get energized? Imagining the exhilarating moment when you take action? Or, did that last question make you nervous? Did it stir up your fears and apprehensions? Don't worry. Fear is perfectly normal. And remember, if you weren't nervous this wouldn't be a true courage challenge, would it? In the next chapter you'll bring those fears out of the dark and into the light so you can get a good look at the obstacles you'll need to overcome with your courage skills.

"Nothing in life is to be feared, it is only to be understood. Now is the time to understand more, so that we can fear less."

—Marie Curie

Chapter 5

WHAT ARE YOU AFRAID OF?

Unfortunately, just knowing what types of courage you'll use to conquer your challenge doesn't magically wipe away any of the fear or anxiety associated with that challenge. Fortunately, you can teach yourself to move around fears and other obstacles in order to achieve a goal you're passionate about achieving.

The first step is bringing everything out into the light. Understanding what you're actually afraid of can help remove the power those fears and obstacles have over you. Here are some examples of typical courage challenge fears:

"I'll lose my job/position/ranking."
"I'll look stupid/be judged by others."
"I'll miss out on something else."
"I'll go bankrupt."
"I'll lose everything I've worked for."
"I'll lose the respect of those around me."
"I did something similar before and got in trouble."
"I'm afraid of the unknown outcome."

EXERCISE 9: WHAT ARE YOU AFRAID OF?

Now it's your turn. What is keeping you from taking action individually, as a team, or within the culture of your organization? Go ahead. Spill it. What's holding you back? Personally, professionally, organizationally. What are the rational or irrational fears that stand between you and the achievement of your objectives?

 My fears (real or imagined) if I go after this challenge are:

Come on – did you get them all? Try writing down three more fears you omitted from the previous page.

EXERCISE 10: WHAT'S YOUR HISTORY WITH FEAR?

Now think back to a couple of times when you went after something that really frightened you. These could be professional or personal challenges (I went skydiving, I switched jobs, I took an international assignment). What were you afraid of when you took the actions? And finally, beyond the simple outcome (I landed safely, I liked my new job, I learned the language) what were the positive effects you felt in your life? What did your courageous acts teach you about yourself?

Courageous act #1:

 What were your fears:

 Positive effects:

Courageous act #2:

 What were your fears:

 Positive effects:

EXERCISE 11: IS COMPLACENCY A FACTOR?

Now, let's talk about complacency. Inertia. Lack of movement. That little voice inside your head that says, *"Eh, why even bother?"* The rationalizing part of your brain that says you're doing fine right where you are. You've acted courageously in the past. Who says you have to keep proving how tough you are? Why risk changing anything?

Complacency comes about for some very good reasons. After all, many, if not most of us, have done well for ourselves by limiting our risks. We've played it safe. We've paid attention to the hierarchies and politics within our organizations. We did what we were taught to do. We colored inside the lines. But staying safe can often translate to staying put. And staying put means you stop growing. Which is one heck of a dangerous way to live your life.

Complacency is one of the toughest hurdles to overcome on your way to a successful courage victory. And, once again, the best way to face your complacency issues is to write them down. On the next page, write down the many ways you have, in your mind, justified not taking action against this particular challenge. Some good examples are phrases like, *"I'm making an okay salary compared to the national average"* or *"There are lots of other people in my same situation"* or *"I don't want to rock the boat in bad economic times."*

 What do you tell yourself to make it okay not to act?

 Now write down two actions you have taken in the past *in spite of* complacency...

EXERCISE 12: PEER PRESSURE/GROUP DYNAMICS

Another powerful barrier to taking action is the fear that comes from what others might say about you or your team when you make your courageous move.

 What criticisms and judgments from others do you fear?

 Now think about the people who would be supportive and even excited by your actions. Who are they and what praise or kudos might you hear from them?

EXERCISE 13: HOW DOES IT FEEL?

Now that you've thought about your fears and taken a realistic look at the barriers, it's time to see how you really feel about your courage challenge. Take a look at your fears from Exercise 9, the positive effects from your past courageous acts from Exercise 10, and the praise or kudos you may receive when you attack your courage challenge.

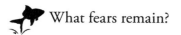 What fears remain?

 Now, consider how those fears stack up against the best possible outcomes you listed for your courage challenge. List the adjectives that describe how you will feel when you succeed.

How could your victory potentially change your life? Your team? Your organization? Your community?

Now look back over all of those ugly little secrets you just wrote down. Are they really and truly valid reasons for not going through with your challenge? What would Albert Einstein, the ultimate rule breaker, have done? What would your favorite business leader or entrepreneur do? What would your personal hero do? The good news is, you're over the hard part, the hump, the heartbreak. Now you're headed for the finish line. Victory is in sight. In the next chapter you'll put all the pieces together. And you'll start with a nugget of wisdom from … Cher!

"Snap out of it!"

—Cher, as Loretta Castorini in the film *Moonstruck*

Chapter 6

How Can You SNAPP Out Of It?

Y ou've got your challenge. You've outlined the possible outcomes. You've worked through the courage types. You've defined your obstacles. Now it's time to put it all together. Remember, courage really isn't about being fearless … it's about taking action in spite of your fear. Very few things in life are 100 percent predictable, no matter how much Core Courage you apply! In the end, whether you succeed or fail, you will have grown. Even failures, real or perceived, will put you one step closer to success. And that will make all your effort worthwhile.

The following simple process is easy to remember by the acronym "SNAPP." This framework can be incredibly useful whether you are working on a large courage challenge or even those day-to-day smaller challenges. In that moment in a meeting when you know you should be speaking up. That moment just before you decide that you really are going to ask for that raise. That moment when you are standing in front of your team describing your vision of success. Whatever that moment is, the SNAPP process can help you move beyond the fear, leap over the barriers, and take action.

EXERCISE 14: SNAPP OUT OF IT

Think about your courage challenge and all the barriers that are keeping you from taking action. The pent up emotions that have you frozen in place.

STOP First, STOP... get the physical under control. Breathe. Take a moment to let your initial anger, frustration, or trepidation pass. Focus on the situation rather than your emotions and the physical ramifications. Stopping allows you to move your reaction from your body and your emotions to your head so you can begin the creative process of dealing with the situation ... rather than just physically responding to it.

 Now, reflect on your courage challenge and describe your physical or emotional reactions and feelings.

Second, NOTICE ... What caused your emotional or physical reaction? Recall the fears, biases, assumptions, and pressures you listed in the previous chapter. Where are those fears coming from? What is the reality behind them? Use the trick you learned earlier and ask yourself why you have those fears or assumptions. Get to the root of what is really creating the fear for you. What is the core issue?

Take the time now to be really honest with yourself. Use the space below to help you get to the root of your fear reaction.

Third, ACT... Now consider the four types of courage and the actions you used to describe how you would employ each type. Choose the action that is most likely to produce the best possible outcome for you, your team, your organization.

Write down the next three steps you need to take to achieve your objective and commit to a schedule or timeframe for taking those steps.

Fourth, PRAISE … Praise yourself and others for taking the action. Praise the friends and colleagues who helped you muster the courage to act and supported you while you did it.

To practice, write a few statements of praise in the space below. Make sure your comments are genuine, heartfelt, and meaningful. Imagine you just won an award for your performance. Who would you thank as the camera clicked away? What would you say?

Fifth, PROCESS … Review the process you followed. What worked and what didn't work. Maybe the overall outcome was a success, but what could you have done faster, better, more expertly? Maybe the overall outcome didn't work the way you had hoped. Look for the bright spots. What good could come of the failure? What did you learn that you didn't know previously? Most importantly, what will you do differently next time?

What went well? How can you take those insights and apply them next time—or to a different courage challenge? How will you make your actions consistent going forward?

What didn't work? What could you do differently next time?

 If you didn't achieve your goal, where are the bright spots? What were the collateral achievements or insights?

Lastly, how did you feel when you were able to consciously choose a courageous action rather than an unconscious reaction?

Now it's time to apply the last two letters of SNAPP to yourself. It's time to accept the accolades you so richly deserve and comb through your process for valuable clues.

"Things are only impossible until they're not."

—Jean-Luc Picard

Chapter 7

YOUR NEXT CHALLENGE

Congratulations! You finished the workbook and attacked your challenge. And you did it equipped with the knowledge and information you needed to taste success. How does it feel? If you are like most people, you gained a bit of confidence from the process. That confidence comes from the new perspective you have on yourself, your team, and/or your organization. It also comes from understanding your fears … and the things you need to do to keep them from getting in your way.

If you're shaking your head – because you didn't succeed in getting that raise, proposing that new idea, or acquiring that competitor – stop yourself! Start seeing even your attempts as successful. And remember, building your courage skills is just like building any other skill. Imagine you're a marathon runner in training. Sometimes, during practice, you'll match or beat the winning record. Other times you'll be way off. But in the end it's the practice, the flexing of your muscles, that will bring about your long-term success.

The simple act of following the framework in this workbook moved your courage skills (or those of your team or your organization) up a notch. By taking the time to work through a challenge from start to finish, you built a foundation. And you began to develop habits that will allow you to take on bigger, more difficult, and even more complex courage challenges from this day forward.

Each time you tackle a new courage challenge, and use SNAPP to work through it, you'll gain more insight and strengthen your courage skills. And, you may notice something else. Your friends, coworkers, colleagues, and higher-ups will start treating you a bit differently—and acting a little more courageous themselves. That's because courage is contagious. You're modeling the behaviors that inspire, motivate, and provide the gentle "push" we all need to become our higher selves.

By taking the time to complete this workbook, you have…

• *Defined New Opportunities*—You thought about your industry, your organization, and your team. And you identified not just one, but probably many opportunities you could tackle over the next few weeks or months.

• *A New Way To Overcome Barriers*—You looked long and hard at the fears and obstacles that hold you back. These same fears are likely to crop up time and time again … but now you are ready for them. So the next time you're in a meeting or faced with a significant career, team, or organizational decision, you can SNAPP away the obstacles and get on with it.

• *Taken Charge Of Courage*—You are more familiar with the four types of courage. You know how to consciously choose which type or types of courage you need to achieve your goals. And you can more readily recognize how others around you are using their courage skills too.

• *Started A Culture Of Courage*—You've already modeled courageous behavior in front of your peers and your team. Demonstrating actions yourself is the number one way to make courage go viral and become an integral part of your organization's culture.

So what's next? You guessed it! Go ahead, choose another courage challenge from your list. Or not from your list. Choose one that will keep your momentum up. One that will help you continue building those courage skills. If you chose an easier one for your first challenge, try a tougher one this time. If you chose a business challenge, try a personal challenge. If you chose a really big one and struggled, go for a smaller one this time around. And remember, practice makes perfect. The more challenges you try, the better you'll get.

Just like that marathon runner. Nobody simply walks out the door one day and runs 26.2 miles. In the same way, you can't realize *all* of your dreams for yourself, your team, your company, or your customers on the very first day. You have to start by running one mile and work up from there. You have to focus on enjoying the good days and taking the not-so-good days in stride. The next thing you know, you'll be crossing the finish line and the paparazzi will be lining up to find out how you did it.

My next courage challenge is...

*"When I let go of what I am,
I become what I might be."*

—Lao Tzu

ACKNOWLEDGMENTS

First, thank you to the (literally) thousands of individuals who have contributed to the insights represented in this workbook either explicitly through participation in *The Leadership Courage Study* or implicitly by attending my keynote presentations and workshops. I owe you all a debt of gratitude for sharing with me your stories and ideas about how we can all create more courage in our lives, in our work, and in businesses.

Secondly, this workbook would not exist if it weren't for the talent, the perseverance, and the generous spirit of my editor and guide, Nancy Holland Hellmrich. Nancy's talent allows me to create more courage in my own life through the terrifying act of "writing it down." Thank you Nancy, for once again allowing me to raise my courage bar even higher.